Incredible Stories of
COURAGE
in sports

BRAD HERZOG

"As shown by the wonderful stories in
Count on Me: Sports, athletics can not only
reveal character, but also inspire it."
—**Shannon Miller**, two-time Olympic gold medalist
in gymnastics

"The true tales in Brad Herzog's books
show how the games we play can teach
seriously important life lessons."
—**Jake Delhomme**, former Super Bowl quarterback
for the Carolina Panthers

free spirit
PUBLISHING®

Library of Congress Cataloging-in-Publication Data
Herzog, Brad.
  Incredible stories of courage in sports / by Brad Herzog.
    pages cm. — (Count on me: Sports)
  Audience: Interest Level Ages: 8–13.
  Includes bibliographical references and index.
  ISBN 978-1-57542-478-1 — ISBN 1-57542-478-9 1. Athletes—Conduct of life—Juvenile literature. 2. Courage—Juvenile literature. 3. Heroes—Juvenile literature. I. Title.
  GV706.3.H465 2014
  306.4'83—dc23
                                                                    2014011994

Free Spirit Publishing does not have control over or assume responsibility for author or third-party websites and their content.

Reading Level Grade 5; Interest Level Ages 8–13;
Fountas & Pinnell Guided Reading Level V

Edited by Alison Behnke
Cover and interior design by Michelle Lee Lagerroos

Cover photo credits: background © Bruxov | Dreamstime.com;
clockwise from top left: AP Photo/Susan Ragan; © Bettmann/Corbis / AP Images; AP Photo/Jeff Chiu; AP Photo; AP Photo/West Hawaii Today, Michael Darden; AP Photo/James Crisp, File.
For interior photo credits, see page 102.

10 9 8 7 6 5 4 3 2 1
Printed in the United States of America
S18860614

Free Spirit Publishing Inc.
Minneapolis, MN
(612) 338-2068
help4kids@freespirit.com
www.freespirit.com

DEDICATION

To the Hanson-Kaplan kids—Josh, Ben, and Josie. And to Adam and Steph—for the courage of their convictions and their companionship.

ACKNOWLEDGMENTS

Thank you to Judy Galbraith, Margie Lisovskis, and the rest of the crew at Free Spirit Publishing for having the courage to pursue a series of books celebrating stories of character in sports. I found Alison Behnke to be both insightful and inclusive as an editor, an author's dream combination, and Michelle Lee Lagerroos put in overtime making sure the designs were just right. Finally, I am grateful to Aimee Jackson for bringing me to Free Spirit in the first place and for her unwavering support and friendship.

CONTENTS

INTRODUCTION

By the winter of 1949, golfer Ben Hogan had won dozens of pro tournaments. But it looked like his career—and maybe his life—would end on a Texas highway. A Greyhound bus swerved to pass a truck. The bus hit Hogan's car head-on. Right before the crash, Hogan threw himself across the passenger seat to shield his wife. She had only minor injuries. He wound up with a broken collarbone, a broken ankle, chipped ribs, and a fractured pelvis.

There were whispers that Hogan would never play golf again. "People have always been telling me what I can't do. I guess I have wanted to show them," he said "That's been one of my driving forces all my life."

Hogan spent 59 days in the hospital. When he got out, he could barely walk. But within a year, Hogan came close to winning a tournament. And just 16 months after the accident, he won the national championship—the U.S. Open. Hogan won five more major tournaments over the next few years. He became one of the top golfers in history.

Hogan's comeback was courageous. So was his instinct to protect his wife. Bravery comes in many forms. And many kinds of bravery can be found in the pages of this book.

Hogan's very best season was in 1953. That year, he won five of the six tournaments he entered. That same year, another all-time great golfer found out she had cancer. Mildred "Babe" Didrikson Zaharias was one of the best athletes ever. She earned two gold medals and a silver medal in track and field at the 1932 Olympics. She also played semi-professional basketball and won tennis and diving championships. Zaharias could even punt a football 75 yards. Then she took up golf. She went on to win 82 amateur and professional tournaments.

After her 1953 cancer diagnosis, Zaharias took time off for treatment. In 1954, she came back and won the U.S. Women's Open. The competition wasn't even close. Zaharias won by an incredible 12 strokes. It was her 10th and final major championship. She died in 1955.

Zaharias had a courageous comeback story. She also displayed another kind of courage—by simply being herself. In her era, people often scorned strong female athletes for being "manly." But Zaharias was proud of her strength and her skills. She kept her hair short. She didn't wear dresses. She was who she was. "It takes courage to grow up and become who you really are," wrote poet e.e. cummings. (And yes, *he* had the courage to spell his name without capital letters.)

The tales in these pages celebrate gutsy sports figures of all kinds. Some—like football player Mike Tepper and horse trainer Boyd Martin—risked their lives to save others. Some faced health issues with grace and dignity, such as baseball great Lou Gehrig and basketball Hall-of-Famer Magic Johnson. Golfer Sophie Gustafson and gymnast Kerri Strug overcame physical challenges in very public ways. Other athletes dared to be different, like basketball forward Rick Barry and hockey goalie Jacques Plante. Still others, including tennis star Billie Jean King and football player Pat Tillman, stood for ideas greater than themselves.

Clearly, sports and courage often go hand in hand. As football great Joe Namath put it, sports can help people find their own strength. "You learn you can do your best even when it's hard, even when you're tired and maybe hurting a little bit," said Namath. "It feels good to show some courage."

BARRIER BREAKER

APRIL 18, 1946 • JERSEY CITY, NEW JERSEY, UNITED STATES

It takes plenty of nerve to face a pitcher throwing a ball 80 or 90 miles per hour. Now just imagine the courage it takes to do it with a nation's eyes upon you. That's what Jackie Robinson did when he carried his bat to home plate on April 18, 1946. One sports writer wrote that on that day, Robinson also carried "the hopes, aspirations, and ambitions of 13 million black Americans."

That April day marked Robinson's first game in baseball's minor leagues. He was playing for the Montreal Royals. This International League team was based in Canada. It had ties to the Brooklyn Dodgers, a U.S. Major League team. Many players were promoted from the Royals to the Dodgers.

When the Royals first announced that Jackie Robinson would play for them, it was big news. For one thing, Robinson was a great athlete. The 26-year-old, who was the grandson of a slave and had served in the U.S. Army, had been a multisport star in college. He'd shown talent in everything from basketball and football to tennis and track and field. Many people said he was one of America's best all-around athletes.

But that wasn't the only reason Robinson made headlines. He had already been a star in the Negro American League. The professional teams in the Negro Leagues featured mostly black players. They had some Hispanic players, too. But for decades, no African-American player had been allowed to compete outside these segregated leagues.

So Robinson was under huge pressure to succeed. Even people who supported baseball's racial integration were worried he might not be talented *enough*. They wondered if he had been picked so he would fail.
Then people who opposed

integration might point to Robinson as an example. They could claim that his poor performance proved black players didn't belong in the minor or major leagues.

On that Opening Day in April 1946, excitement was high. A sellout crowd of 52,000 people filled a ballpark in Jersey City, New Jersey. They were eager to see just what Robinson could do.

"We all sensed that history was in the making," Robinson later wrote. "The long ban on Negro players was about to come crashing down, setting up reverberations that would echo across a continent and perhaps around the world."

In his first at-bat against the Jersey City Giants, Robinson grounded out to the shortstop. But in his next trip to the plate, he sent a fastball soaring into the left-field stands. It was a three-run homer. George Shuba was one of Robinson's Montreal teammates. He shook his hand after Robinson rounded the bases. Shuba recalled, "You could see in his face how happy he was. You could see he was overwhelmed with joy."

And Robinson wasn't done. That day, he racked up four hits, four runs, three runs batted in, and two stolen bases. Montreal beat Jersey City 14–1. "I couldn't have dreamed up a better start," Robinson said. He had shown the world that he was the right man for this challenge. As one observer put it, "He did everything but help the ushers seat the crowd."

Robinson went on to bat .349 that season. He led the International League in hitting for the year. Robinson's performance was even more impressive considering the fact that he missed 30 games due to injuries. (Some opponents purposely cut him with the spikes on their shoes. Others threw pitches that hit him.) Yet he scored more runs (113) than any other player in the International League and stole 40 bases. The Royals competed in the 1946 Junior World Series, the postseason series between the top minor league champions. Robinson's team defeated the American Association's Louisville Colonels.

The next season, Robinson made history again when he became a major leaguer as a Brooklyn Dodger. He scored 125 runs and led the league with 29 stolen bases. Robinson was named the 1947 National League Rookie of the Year.

Jackie Robinson had arrived. So had baseball's integration. In 1962, Robinson was voted into the National Baseball Hall of Fame. He'd had 10 amazing big league seasons. But it all started with what might have been the most important hit in baseball history. "It was the exclamation, that home run," said Shuba. "It was the knockout punch."

A WELCOMING GESTURE

Jackie Robinson performed under incredible stress as the first black player in the National League. Not much later—in July 1947—another man faced an equally tough task. Centerfielder Larry Doby joined the Cleveland Indians. He was the first black player in the American League.

Doby went on to be a seven-time all-star. But when he first met his teammates, some of them refused to even shake his hand. During warm-ups before his first game, he stood alone. Finally one of the team's longtime players, second baseman Joe Gordon, asked him to play catch. The two men became close friends. Eventually, both were elected to the Hall of Fame.

BRAVE IN THE WAVES

NOVEMBER 2003 • KAUAI, HAWAII, UNITED STATES

Halloween morning in 2003 started like many other days for 13-year-old Bethany Hamilton. She went to Tunnels Beach to meet her best friend Alana and Alana's family. The beach is on the North Shore of the Hawaiian island of Kauai. Together, Hamilton and her friend surfed.

Hamilton had been standing on surfboards almost since she could stand up at all. She dreamed of being a professional surfer someday. In fact, she had won her first surfing competition at the age of eight. She had a bright future catching waves.

But that morning, Hamilton's life changed forever. She was resting on her surfboard. She dangled her left arm in the water. Suddenly, a 14-foot-long tiger shark attacked her. It happened very quickly. All Hamilton saw was a gray blur. The shark took a chunk out of her surfboard. It also took her left arm.

Hamilton's friends rushed to her aid. They helped her paddle to shore. Alana's father grabbed a surfboard leash. (This cord connects a surfboard to the surfer's leg.) He wrapped the leash tightly around the stump of Hamilton's arm. That slowed down the bleeding. In fact, it probably saved Hamilton's life. Still, by the time she got to the hospital, Hamilton had lost more than 60 percent of her blood. Her father was supposed to have knee surgery that day. Instead, Hamilton took his place in the operating room. "It was just a miracle that I survived," she later recalled.

Soon her thoughts turned to her future. *What am I going to do?* she wondered. "All of these ideas were popping up," she said. "But inside, I knew that I wanted to at least try surfing again."

It took a lot of courage to get back in the water after such an ordeal. But Hamilton says she wasn't that afraid of another shark attack. She was more worried about the physical challenge. Could she still do what she loved? She and her family weren't sure. "We had never heard of anyone surfing with one arm," she explained. "We didn't know if it was possible."

Only three weeks after she'd almost died, Hamilton paddled out into the ocean again. She struggled at first. She tried—and failed—to catch two waves. With only one arm, it was very hard to stand up on the surfboard and keep her balance as she got into the right position.

COURAGEOUS CAMEL

Jeff "Camel" Goulden is an Australian surfer. He's well known for his daring. He had tested some of the biggest waves off Western Australia. But in August 2012, he showed a completely different kind of courage. Goulden was nearby when a surfer was attacked twice by a shark. The surfer defended himself, punching the shark in the snout after the first attack. But he was badly injured. And the shark was still out there. So Goulden swam to the bleeding man and helped him safely to shore. As a local surfer put it, "If you need someone to paddle you away from a shark, Camel is it."

But then she caught the third wave and rode it all the way in. Hamilton cried tears of joy. "Once I did it," she said, "I knew I was going to be doing it for a long time."

By January 2004, Hamilton was ready to get back to competition. In her very first event, she placed fifth. That year she also won a Best Comeback Athlete award from ESPN. In 2005, she was first in her division at the National Scholastic Surfing Association National Championships.

Before long, Hamilton had achieved her dream of becoming a pro surfer. At the same time, she inspired millions of people. She wrote a book titled *Soul Surfer* about her experiences. Soon the book became a movie. Hamilton did many of the film's surfing stunts herself. She also founded Friends of Bethany. This charity supports amputees and people who have survived shark attacks. And she has traveled the world, spreading her message. Hamilton tells people to have faith that they can reach their goals. She urges them not to give up. "Just go out there," she said, "and do it."

VAULT INTO HISTORY

JULY 23, 1996 • ATLANTA, GEORGIA, UNITED STATES

For nearly 40 years, the Russian women's gymnastics squads had dominated Olympic team competition. Things were different at the 1996 Summer Olympics in Atlanta, Georgia. That year, the U.S. team knew it had a chance.

The best-known American gymnasts on that 1996 squad were Shannon Miller, Dominique Moceanu, and Dominique Dawes. A less famous team member was 18-year-old Kerri Strug. She was tiny—just 4 feet and 9 inches tall. But she was tough.

For years, Strug had practiced six or seven days a week. Often she lived away from her family so she could train with top coaches. But on that warm night in July, her parents were close by. They were sitting in the crowd at the stadium in Atlanta. And they

15

watched nervously as a nation pinned its hopes on their daughter.

Going into the last part of the team competition, the Americans held a lead over the Russians. All they had left was the vault. Unfortunately, the first four U.S. gymnasts struggled with their vaults. Moceanu fell twice, earning a low score. A hush fell over the crowd. Strug was the last to go. "My heart was beating like crazy," she recalled. "It was now up to me." She tried to calm her nerves. *You've done this vault a thousand times*, she thought to herself.

On Strug's first try, she landed badly and fell. Her score was only 9.162. Even worse, she had sprained her left ankle. She wasn't sure if she could take her second vault.

Strug was no stranger to coping with injuries. Two years earlier, she had lost her grip on the uneven bars. She'd flown off the high bar and landed in a twisted position on the mat. One of her back muscles was badly pulled. Yet she returned to gymnastics six months later. This time, Strug was being asked to return from an injury just *moments* after it happened.

"Do we need this?" she asked her coach, Bela Karolyi. He believed they did. He told her she needed to land a strong second vault for the team to clinch the gold. "You can do it," he said. Strug nodded. "This is the Olympics. This is what you dream about from when you're five years old," she later explained. "I wasn't going to stop."

Strug limped to the end of the vault runway for her second attempt. She took a deep breath.

FINISHING FIRST

At the 2012 Summer Olympics in London, Manteo Mitchell was part of a relay team. Together, they were running the 4x400-meter race. It would determine which teams made it to the finals. Mitchell was the first runner in the relay.

Mitchell started strong. Suddenly, about halfway toward passing the baton to his teammate, he heard a loud pop. Actually, he later said, "I heard it and I felt it." Afterward, doctors told Mitchell he had broken a bone in his left leg. As he kept running, he was in a lot of pain. But he wanted to finish his job for the team. "Even though track is an individual sport, you've got three guys depending on you," Mitchell said about his relay teammates. "You don't want to let anyone down." So he finished his lap. Then he limped to the side of the track. Mitchell watched the rest of the Olympics while leaning on crutches. His courage paid off, though. In this race, the Americans tied for first place.

Then she ran at full speed down the runway. She did a back handspring, launching herself off the springboard and onto the vault. Next she sprang off the vault and did a move in the air called a one-and-a-half-twist Yurchenko. And *then*, she landed on her feet. The crowd burst into applause.

Almost instantly, Strug started hopping on one leg. She couldn't stand on her left foot. She collapsed onto her knees. "Kerri Strug is hurt! She is hurt badly," cried a TV announcer. "Probably the last thing she should have done was vault again, but she did. And now she is in a lot of pain."

Strug's injuries would keep her from competing in the individual competitions. But her final vault earned a score of 9.712. That was what her team needed to beat the Russians. Strug couldn't walk on her ankle. So Karolyi carried her to the medal podium for the National Anthem. Minutes later, Strug was standing with her teammates. She had a bandage around her ankle—and a gold medal around her neck.

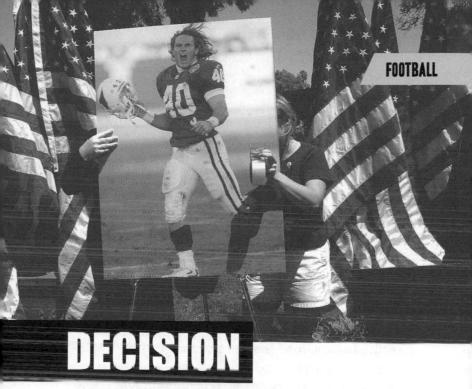

DECISION

APRIL 8, 2002 • PHOENIX, ARIZONA, UNITED STATES

Not every story of courage has a happy ending. But each is a tale of heroic feats. Pat Tillman may have been the ultimate athlete-hero.

Tillman was a football player. But he was far more than that. He starred as a linebacker at Arizona State University and earned conference Player of the Year honors in 1997. He also recorded nearly straight A's and graduated with honors in only three and a half years. He set a team record for tackles while playing

19

strong safety for the Arizona Cardinals in 2000. And during the off-season, he volunteered for charities and studied history at Arizona State.

Tillman was also an avid reader who liked to debate politics. He thought deeply about many issues. He loved football and believed the game taught meaningful lessons. But he felt he needed to do more in life. That feeling got stronger after the terrorist attacks on September 11, 2001, which killed almost 3,000 Americans. Nearly seven months later, on April 8, 2002, Tillman sat down at a computer and started typing. The title of what he wrote was "Decision."

Tillman explained that he and his girlfriend, Marie, were getting married one month later. "We have a great life," he wrote. "However, it is not enough. These last few years, and especially after recent events, I've come to appreciate just how shallow and insignificant my role is. I'm no longer satisfied with the path I've been following." He closed the essay by writing, "My voice is calling me in a different direction. It is up to me whether or not to listen."

Tillman was 25 years old at the time. He was likely at the peak of his athletic powers. In fact, the Cardinals offered him a three-year contract for more than one million dollars per season. He turned it down. How many people would have the courage to do that? Instead, shortly after his honeymoon with Marie, Tillman joined the U.S. Army. He told his younger brother Kevin, a minor league baseball player, about his plans. Kevin joined, too.

Tillman loved the United States. But his decision wasn't just about patriotism. Several members of his family had fought in World War II and the Korean War. One had been the last man to jump out of a crashing airplane. As a highly paid pro athlete, Tillman knew he had benefited from others' sacrifices. He also knew that others had to work very hard for less than he had. So he opted to take on hard work, too. And he didn't do it for the publicity. Tillman never did a single interview about his decision.

Tillman joined the Army Rangers. He served two tours in combat. On April 22, 2004, in the mountains of Afghanistan, he was shot. Fellow U.S. soldiers mistakenly fired toward Tillman's location. Those soldiers thought they were being attacked by the enemy. Tillman was hit. He died instantly.

LOYAL TO THE END

Tillman didn't start out a football star. In fact, he was picked near the end of the college draft. Finally the Arizona Cardinals chose him—226th out of 241 players taken. Later, the Seattle Seahawks offered him a huge long-term contract. Tillman turned it down. He was loyal to the team that had taken a chance on him. In December 2003, the Seahawks offered him another contract. At that point, Tillman was with the Army. The Seahawks were offering him a chance to return to football. The team had discovered that he could be released from the remainder of his three-year Army contract because he had served in a war zone. Tillman refused again. This time, he said no out of loyalty to the Army. "I owe them three years," he said. "I'm not going back on my word."

Seven months later, Arizona State University played its last home game of the season. During that game, the school retired Tillman's jersey number, 42. Students painted his number on their backs. The school band formed a 42 on the field. Even the opposing players wore the initials PT on their helmets. One group of fans brought a homemade poster to the game. It showed a drawing of Tillman. Next to it were seven words that said it all: "To remind us what courage looks like."

SAVING NEVILLE

MAY 30, 2011 • COCHRANVILLE, PENNSYLVANIA, UNITED STATES

It was just after midnight on Memorial Day in 2011 when Boyd Martin got a phone call. The panicked voice on the line had bad news. There was a fire in the stables. Horses were trapped inside.

Martin didn't waste any time. He sprinted to his car and drove the 6 miles to Pennsylvania's True Prospect Farm. When he got there, he saw a barn engulfed in flames.

Firefighters were already on the scene. They said the building was close to collapsing. It was too dangerous to go in. "I'm real sorry," said the fire chief. "Everything's gone." But Martin refused to give up. He shouted and struggled. Finally he got past the firefighters. He rushed to the barn door.

Martin was the son of two former Winter Olympians. His mother was an American speed skater, and his father was an Australian cross-country skier. Martin was raised in Australia around horses. At a young age, he fell in love with the sport of horseback riding.

Martin competed in eventing. Eventing is like an equestrian triathlon. The first part is dressage. In this section, the horse and rider perform a precise series of movements. Dressage tests a horse's obedience and connection with the rider. Next is the cross-country segment. In cross-country, the horse gallops through an outdoor course filled with jumps and other obstacles. The third portion is show jumping. It also takes the horse and rider over a series of jumps. This time, the course is inside. In all three parts of eventing, the bond of trust between the rider and the horse is very important.

In 2003, still living in Australia, Martin heard about a three-year-old, chestnut-colored horse that was too slow for the racetrack. The horse was named Neville Bardos. He was half-American and half-Australian, just like Martin. Martin bought Neville for only $850 and probably saved his life. (Sometimes owners kill racehorses that don't perform well.)

At first, Martin wondered if he'd made a mistake. Neville turned out to be "a bit of a handful," Martin recalled. In fact, in one early event, Neville got spooked and ran away. It took 15 minutes to catch him. But over time, horse and rider developed a strong bond. Success followed. In 2007, the pair moved to the United States. By 2010, at the World Equestrian Games, Neville was the top American horse.

After all that, Martin wasn't going to let *anyone* stop him from rushing into the fiery barn to save Neville Bardos. "It's not like I'm going in there to save a motorcycle," he said later. "It's a living, breathing partner in your sport."

LOVE CONQUERS ALL

Patrick Downes and Jessica Kensky were newlyweds. On April 15, 2013, they were watching the Boston Marathon. They had a great spot—right near the finish line. Suddenly a bomb exploded nearby. Chaos followed. Downes and Kensky were both badly hurt.

The husband and wife survived. But both of them lost their left legs. A year later, Downes spoke at a ceremony on the anniversary of the tragedy. He celebrated the people who saved his life and those of his wife and others. "We chose to love," he said, "and that has made all the difference." Six days after his speech, Downes and Kensky competed in the 2014 Boston Marathon's handcycle division. They used their upper bodies to power special cycles. And they crossed the finish line together, holding hands.

When Martin got inside, the barn was full of thick black smoke. It was almost impossible to see anything. But Martin heard a horse struggling for breath. He felt his way around until he found Neville. The horse was black with burns and soot. He was so scared that he wouldn't budge. Fortunately, Martin wasn't alone. Phillip Dutton was a former Olympic gold medalist in horseback riding. He owned the farm and rented the stables to Martin. Dutton had followed him in. Together, they managed to get Neville outside. Four other horses also survived the fire. Six died.

When Martin saw Neville later at the veterinary hospital, the horse was hooked up to all kinds of tubes and machines. Neville's throat was burned all the way to his lungs. Martin figured that he and Neville would never compete together again. "We were happy he was alive," he said. Martin didn't hope for much more than that.

But Neville surprised everyone. He healed quickly. Only three months after the fire, the horse-and-rider duo took part in England's Burghley Horse Trials. It was an important competition. Martin and Neville finished seventh. The following summer, they were both members of the U.S. Olympic team.

Martin went through hard times after the barn fire. He had lost many of his prized horses. And, only a few weeks later, his father died after a bicycle accident. But Neville's recovery helped Martin recover, too. Martin said, "We're lucky we both found each other."

MAGIC MOMENT

FEBRUARY 9, 1992 • ORLANDO, FLORIDA, UNITED STATES

There were just 20 seconds left in the 1992 NBA All-Star Game. Earvin "Magic" Johnson had the ball. The shot clock was ticking down. And everybody in the Orlando, Florida, stadium waited for what was coming next. Johnson dribbled to his right. He made sure his feet were behind the three-point line. Then he lofted an off-balance shot. This was just an exhibition game. It didn't matter to anybody's team record. But in some ways, Johnson's shot was one of his most important ever.

Three months earlier, Johnson had stood at a podium with cameras flashing all around him. The 6-foot-9 point guard had won five championships with the Los Angeles Lakers. He would retire as the NBA's all-time career assist leader. He was known as "Magic" for both his play and his personality. It is possible that there has never been a more beloved basketball player than Magic Johnson. That's partly why his public statement on November 7, 1991, stunned people around the world. He announced that he had HIV. It's the virus that causes AIDS.

Johnson was still a great player. He had starred in the NBA Finals just five months earlier. But he said he was retiring from basketball immediately.

Some athletes might have been tempted to hide their illness. At the time, most people thought that HIV would definitely turn into AIDS. There is no cure for AIDS yet. Sadly, fans expected Magic Johnson to die soon.

But Johnson had other ideas. He said, "I plan on going on living for a *long* time." Johnson decided to become a spokesperson in the battle against the disease. He started the Magic Johnson Foundation. It has raised more than $10 million for HIV/AIDS research and charities. Johnson also helped create a television show and a book to teach kids about the disease.

One moment in particular showed that Johnson's mission was working. He was reminding the world that people with HIV could thrive. In February 1992, NBA fans voted him to a spot on the Western Conference all-star squad. (They didn't seem to care that he'd retired.) In a show of respect, Golden State Warriors guard Tim Hardaway gave up his starting spot. He let Johnson take his place. Then the popular player put on a magical show.

In the last few minutes of the game, Johnson had already made two three-point shots and two fantastic passes. He would finish with 25 points and 9 assists. That was more than anyone else in the game. As a defender, he had even gone one-on-one against the great Michael Jordan, causing Jordan to miss his shot. Now, with only seconds left in the game, Johnson got the ball back. He launched that final three-pointer and . . . *swish!*

The crowd roared. There was still time left on the clock, but everyone knew that was how the game should end. Players on both teams ran up to Johnson with wide smiles on their faces. They high-fived and hugged him. "You can't orchestrate it better

"All kids need is a little help, a little hope, and somebody who believes in them."
—Magic Johnson

than that!" said TV announcer Dick Enberg. The West beat the East 153–113, and Johnson was named the game's Most Valuable Player.

Magic Johnson would actually return to basketball. He starred on the famous U.S. Dream Team that won gold at the 1992 Olympics. He also played in 36 games for the Lakers after coming out of retirement in 1995. Plus, in the two decades after his historic announcement, he grew famous not just as an athlete or even as a survivor. He also became a successful businessman, owning many coffee shops and movie theaters. And in 2012, he became a partial owner of the Los Angeles Dodgers baseball team. Still, that one all-star game was extra-special. Johnson said, "That was the therapy I needed to continue to live the rest of my life."

ALL-OUT EFFORT

NOVEMBER 2, 2013 • KERNERSVILLE, NORTH CAROLINA, UNITED STATES

Imagine finding out you have a disease with no cure. You learn that someday this disease might keep you in a wheelchair. Imagine that you love to run, but when you do, your legs go completely numb. In a race, you'll collapse at the finish line—every time. What would you do?

Kayla Montgomery didn't have to imagine. She faced this decision in real life. What did *she* do? "Instead of letting it stop me from running," she said, "I've used it to motivate me to break records."

When Montgomery was 15, she fell while playing soccer. As she lay on the ground, she realized that she temporarily couldn't feel her legs. The same thing happened while she competed on Mount Tabor High School's cross-country team.

Montgomery went to the doctor to find out what was wrong. She got shocking news. She had multiple sclerosis. The disease causes balance problems and muscle weakness. In severe cases, it even causes paralysis.

MS (as it is often called) blocks nerve signals from the brain to the rest of the body. This is especially true during intense exercise. When Montgomery races, she starts out feeling normal. But after about a mile, her legs gradually go numb. She can keep moving forward at a steady speed. But any change in her movement— especially stopping or falling—makes her lose control of her legs. "When I finish, it feels like there's nothing underneath me," she said. She staggers and crumples to the ground.

At Mount Tabor, Montgomery and the people who care about her set up a routine. During

WISE WORDS

"A winner is a person who gets up one more time than she is knocked down."

—Mia Hamm, soccer legend and two-time Olympic gold medalist

races, her coach, Patrick Cromwell, waited at the finish line. He braced to catch her as she fell. He then carried her to the side of the track. Her parents waited there, ready to ice her legs. Eventually, the feeling in her legs would return. And every time, Montgomery got up again.

Another amazing thing? Often, Montgomery was the first one across the finish line. When she was first diagnosed with MS, Montgomery was one of her team's slower runners. She told her coach, "I don't know how much time I have left, so I want to run fast—don't hold back." Soon her times started getting better. This may have been partly because the numbness lets her ignore pain that other runners feel. But it was also because of her attitude. Her challenge gave her new determination. In fact, on November 2, 2013, Montgomery won the North Carolina state cross-country championship. That was during the fall of her senior year. A few months later, she won the 3,200-meter indoor title.

Still, Montgomery always collapsed at the end. At the national indoor 5,000-meter championships during her junior year, officials forgot to catch her. She fell facedown and had to wait for someone to carry her away. At the state cross-country meet that year, she caught the heel of a fellow runner. Montgomery crashed to the ground. At first, she couldn't get up. Runners passed her by. So she used a nearby fence to pull herself back to her feet. And then she started running again.

"Now I know I can do it," said Montgomery. "It may take a little while, but if I fall, I know I can get up."

KICK START

SEPTEMBER 4, 2004 • BATON ROUGE, LOUISIANA, UNITED STATES

It isn't easy to be a placekicker in football. It takes guts. You're only on the field briefly during each game. And every time, you're under a massive amount of pressure. Sure, you get credit when you're successful. But you get even more blame when you mess up.

Just ask Alexis Serna. In 2004, he was a freshman at Oregon State University. And his very first game as placekicker was on national television. The OSU

Beavers were playing the Louisiana State Tigers. The Tigers were the defending national champions. That day, Serna missed three extra points, including one in overtime. OSU lost by a single point.

It's often said that people can be measured by how they react to defeat. Several of Serna's teammates didn't react very well. They yelled at the 5-foot-7 kicker as he sat in the locker room with tears in his eyes. Many fans behaved poorly, too. One sent Serna an email that said, "Your parents are embarrassed of you." (Do you think maybe *that* person's parents might be embarrassed?)

But Serna also received hundreds of letters of support. One of them made all the difference.

Twelve-year-old Austan Pierce was being treated for cancer in Spokane, Washington. After watching the OSU game on television, he wrote to Serna. "Sorry you had such an awful day in Louisiana. I've had some bad days myself," Pierce wrote. "But the most important thing is to get up again and do what you know what you can do. If I can do it, so can you."

Serna got Pierce's note just after the coach had benched him for a game. "What Austan said helped me put football and life into perspective," he recalled. "For a boy who has already endured more pain and hurt at age 12 than most of us will ever experience in

our lifetime, Austan is as courageous as they come."

When Serna returned to the field for his next game, he wrote "A" on one thumb and "P" on the other. The letters reminded him of Austan Pierce's courage. In the fourth quarter, Serna tried for a field goal . . . and made it. Over the next few months, Serna and Pierce exchanged emails and phone calls. Serna also sent a package to Pierce that included a hat, a shirt, and tickets to an OSU game. Some generous Oregon fans heard about the story. They wanted to help. So they paid for Pierce and his family to travel to the game. With his new pal watching, Serna made three field goals in the first half.

Pierce still faced tough times. Doctors had to amputate one of his legs because of the cancer. But Pierce continued to live with courage. He went on to be an honors student. He also became a wheelchair basketball star at the University of Texas at Arlington.

Meanwhile, Serna became the greatest kicker in Oregon State history. He made 144 extra points in a row—an OSU record. He set another school record by making six field goals in one game. Serna won the Lou Groza Award as the nation's top kicker and went on to play in the Canadian Football League. For the rest of his career, he wrote "A" and "P" on his thumbs on game day. "My football career is in the past, but my relationship with Austan is something that is always continuing," he said later. "I have a friend for life."

FIRST LADY

FEBRUARY 2014 • SOCHI, RUSSIA

It shouldn't have been a big deal. Before the 2014 Winter Olympics, President Barack Obama chose three former athletes to join the U.S. Olympic Team in Sochi, Russia. These athletes led a delegation—a group representing the United States at the Games. But it *was* a big deal. Because all three of those athletes are gay. And Russia had recently passed a law that threatened gay rights there. President Obama was making a statement. He was saying: The United States supports the equality of all people—gay or straight, male or female, of any race or religion.

Billie Jean King won a lot of points on the tennis court during her Hall of Fame career. She was also devoted to pointing out injustice and inequality beyond sports. So it was natural that President Obama chose her to go to Sochi. The trip had risks. If King said something in support of gay rights, Russian police could arrest her. She could even be thrown in jail. Still, King was unafraid. She simply said, "I'll take that chance."

King was no stranger to taking a chance. More than 40 years earlier, on September 20, 1973, she took a big one. She competed in a tennis match that came to be known as the "Battle of the Sexes."

The event was unlike any in tennis before—or after. More than 30,000 fans filled the Houston Astrodome. Nearly 50 million people in 37 countries were glued to their television sets. And King had a huge weight on her shoulders. She represented the pride and purpose of 51 percent of the population. It was just a tennis match. And it was a pretty silly match, at that. But she knew that if she didn't win, the world might see it as more than just a sporting loss.

In 1973, King was the queen of women's tennis. She had been the world's top-ranked player for most of the previous seven years. She'd won dozens of Grand Slam championships. And she was more than a great competitor. She believed deeply that female athletes deserved equal opportunity, equal prize money, and equal respect. She fought for those things during the struggle for women's rights in the 1960s, 1970s, and beyond. She started the Women's Sports Foundation to promote athletic opportunities for girls and women. And one of her most important battles for women's rights came on the tennis court.

Bobby Riggs had been the world's top player three decades earlier. By 1973, he was 55 years old. His game had slowed down. That didn't stop him from talking a big game, though. Riggs claimed that women didn't deserve equal prize money. He also said that the top female players couldn't beat men—even an older man like him. So King, then 29 years old, agreed to compete against him.

The match took place in late September. Lots of silliness surrounded the event. King was brought onto the court on a throne carried by four men. Riggs showed up in a rickshaw pulled by six women. The players even exchanged gifts before the match. Riggs gave King a gigantic lollipop. King gave Riggs a baby pig. But silly or not, King knew a victory could boost the self-esteem of women around the globe. "It was not about tennis. It was about social change," she said. "It was about changing a way of thinking, about getting women athletes accepted."

Most people expected Riggs to win. Four months earlier, he had played top women's player Margaret Court. In two sets, he beat her 6–2 and 6–1. But King was determined not to lose. In their three-set match, she ran Riggs all over the court. She won in three straight sets—6–4, 6–3, 6–3. When it was over, she joyfully flung her racket into the air. Riggs leaped over the net. He hugged King and told her, "You were too good." Later, he told reporters, "I said a lot of things. I was wrong. I admit it."

Seventeen years later, in 1990, King was inducted into the National Women's Hall of Fame. That same year, *Life* magazine named her one of the 100 most important Americans of the 20th century. And in 2009, she was awarded the Presidential Medal of Freedom.

Martina Navratilova is another female tennis legend. She described how King had inspired thousands of female athletes and millions of women, including her. She said, "Billie Jean was a crusader, fighting a battle for all of us."

"WE'RE SOCIETY, TOO"

In 1981, Martina Navratilova was at the top of her game. She was perhaps the greatest female tennis player in history. That year, she faced a moment of truth. She wanted to *tell* the truth. She knew that some people would react negatively. Even so, she had the courage to publicly announce that she was gay. She was the first superstar to do so *while* she was a superstar, not after her career had ended. Donna Lopiano, former chief executive of the Women's Sports Foundation, spoke about Navratilova's decision. Lopiano explained, "She basically said this part of my life doesn't have anything to do with me as a tennis player. Judge me for who I am." Later, Navratilova recalled that a friend had once told her that society wasn't ready to accept gay and lesbian athletes. Navratilova's response? "We're society, too."

FREE SPIRIT

1960s AND 1970s • UNITED STATES

"Failure is unimportant," the great silent-film actor Charlie Chaplin once said. "It takes courage to make a fool of yourself." Chaplin *did* often make himself look silly. But he was also one of the best ever at what he did. He was a comedian who loved to make people laugh. You could say the same thing about Hall of Fame basketball player Rick Barry. Except Barry didn't really care whether people laughed at him.

Barry was named one of the 50 greatest players in NBA history. During the 1960s and 1970s, he was an all-star 12 times. He averaged 24.8 points per game and won many big awards. But he was especially famous for his free throw shooting. When he retired, he was the all-time leader in the category. During his career, he made nearly 90 percent of his free throw shots.

Every time Barry stood at the foul line, he followed exactly the same pattern. First, he got his feet into a

comfortable position. Then he bent low and bounced the ball three times. Not once. Not twice. Repetition, he always said, was the key. "It's the same way, time after time after time, so it's something that gets embedded in your mind," he explained. So far, his routine wasn't very unusual. But the next part was. He let his arms hang down to his waist. And then he tossed the ball *underhanded* toward the basket.

"Granny style" is what people called it, and it didn't look all that cool. Still, it worked for Barry. Another top player, Wilt Chamberlain, tried it once. He averaged more than 30 points per game in his career. Yet he made barely half of his foul shots. His free throw shooting was so bad that he gave Barry's method a chance. But he soon stopped. His reason? "I felt silly."

Barry felt the same way when he was younger. His father coached a semi-pro basketball team. He always tried to get his son to shoot the ball underhanded. That's how most players had done it in basketball's early days. But Barry refused at first. He was afraid people would make fun of him during games.

"See, that's the problem," said Al Attles, who later coached Barry in the NBA. "If you worry about what people feel or think, you're going to have a problem. You have to do whatever is the best way to make the ball go in the basket."

Still, it takes courage to risk being mocked. Finally, as a high school junior, Barry decided to test out the underhanded style. During a road game he shot his first free throws this way. Sure enough, someone in the crowd taunted him. But then Barry heard another man in the crowd say, "What are you making fun of him for? He doesn't miss." Soon, Barry was shooting *only* underhanded free throws. "It's the first time I ever shot 80 percent," he said. "Then I just kept getting better."

Barry's goal was to relax as much as possible at the line. His underhanded method helped him do that because his arms were in a natural position. It also allowed him to put backspin on the ball. Backspin makes the ball more likely to fall through the hoop even after bouncing on the rim. Also, most free throw shooters use mostly one hand to guide the ball. But Barry used both hands to direct its flight. "I think I have much more opportunity to shoot the ball accurately," he explained. Indeed, twice in his career, he shot 18 free throws in a game and made every single one of them. Once, he made 60 foul shots in a row.

So why doesn't anyone else shoot that way? "Ego is the only reason nobody will even try it anymore," said Barry. But he was willing to brave the mockery of the rest in order to be the best. After all, he said, "What's it matter what you look like when the ball is going in the basket?"

TOP FLOP

Around the time Rick Barry turned pro, another world-class athlete was mocked for doing things differently. By 1963, almost every high jumper in the world used a style called the Straddle. They leaped over the bar with their legs straddling it, and went over the bar face down. But that method just didn't work for 15-year-old Dick Fosbury. Instead, he jumped shoulders first, with his face toward the sky. Then he arched his back as he went over the bar. People thought he looked ridiculous. They said he reminded them of a fish flopping into a boat. One newspaper headline even called him the "WORLD'S LAZIEST HIGH JUMPER." But within a few years, Fosbury was the top college high jumper in the United States. In 1968 he won an Olympic gold medal. By 1980, nearly every Olympic finalist was using his style. They called it the Fosbury Flop.

LEAGUE LEADERS

NOVEMBER 7, 1973 • HOBOKEN, NEW JERSEY, UNITED STATES

Sometimes major change is the result of many smaller courageous acts.

In the spring of 1972, there was an excellent baseball player in Hoboken, New Jersey. Nearly every day, 11-year-old Maria Pepe played the game with her cousins and their friends. When it was time to sign up for Little League tryouts, however, she waited outside while the boys signed up. She wasn't sure if she was even allowed to go in. But the boys wanted her to have a chance. They told the coach, Jimmy Farina, that they needed one more tryout form. The form was for Pepe. So what if she was a girl? She was good! That was Courageous Act #1.

Farina walked outside. He asked the shy girl if she wanted to try out. That was Courageous Act #2.

Pepe made the team. Her family didn't have much money. But her father found enough to pay for cleats. Her grandfather bought her a new glove. She played— and played very well. But some people weren't happy about the girl in the number 9 jersey. Coaches and parents of kids on other teams began to protest. Soon Farina got a call from Little League headquarters in Williamsport, Pennsylvania. Official Little League Baseball rules said that only boys ages 8 to 12 could play. The organization demanded that Farina take Pepe off the team. Farina refused. (Courageous Act #3.) League officials then told him that if he didn't follow the rule, nobody in Hoboken

would be allowed to play.
So only three games into
her Little League career,
Pepe decided it wasn't
worth the risk to her
friends. Brokenhearted, she
turned in her uniform.

"MARIA PEPE KICKED
OFF TEAM," read a local
newspaper headline. The news upset people at the
National Organization for Women (NOW). NOW filed
a lawsuit on Pepe's behalf. (That was Courageous Act
#4.) The lawsuit said that Little League was discrimi-
nating against Pepe because of her gender.

Sylvia Pressler from the New Jersey Civil Rights
Division was assigned to judge the case. On November
7, 1973, she returned with her decision. She wrote,
"Little League is as American as the hot dog and apple
pie. There is no reason why that part of Americana
should be withheld from girls." (Courageous Act #5.)

Unfortunately, by the time the case ended, Pepe
was too old for Little League. She later played college softball. But she admitted, "If I had one wish, it
would be to be able to go back and play those couple
of years." Still, while she never got the chance to play
organized baseball, she helped change it forever.

The national Little League office soon faced similar lawsuits. Finally, the organization decided to change its rules to welcome girls. Since then, more than 10 million girls have played Little League Softball. Thousands more have played Little League Baseball.

Three decades after these courageous acts, Pepe got an unexpected phone call. She was asked to throw out the first pitch at the 2004 Little League World Series. The league also asked to display Pepe's old cap and glove at the organization's museum in Williamsport.

When Pepe got to Williamsport, a man named Creighton Hale asked to meet her. Hale was a former Little League executive. He was one of the people who had kept Pepe from playing all those years ago. For Hale and Pepe to meet after such a troubled history took courage, too. Hale tried to express his appreciation for Pepe's positive role in that history. He told her simply, "My granddaughter plays." Without Maria Pepe, that might not have been possible.

FINISHING STRONG

MAY 16, 2010 • BERKELEY, CALIFORNIA, UNITED STATES

The eight members of the University of California, Berkeley women's crew gripped their oars tightly. They sat facing one much smaller member of the team—5-foot-4-inch Jill Costello. Without a doubt, she was the strongest of the bunch. The team's race for their conference championship was about to begin. As they got ready, the rowers thought about the challenges Costello had already faced. Their task was simple in comparison.

Costello was perfect for the role of coxswain. This lightweight member of the crew is the only one facing forward. She's also the only one without an oar. It's the coxswain's job to steer the boat and keep all eight rowers moving together. She's the motivator on the water. And Costello's story was enough to motivate anybody.

The summer before her senior year, Costello had been stunned by terrible news. She had lung cancer.

57

Costello was 50 years younger than the average lung cancer patient. But doctors told her that she probably had only nine months to live. When she asked about rejoining the Cal crew, the doctors thought she was crazy. Her cancer treatments would be very hard. They would take a toll on her body and her energy.

Still, Costello was determined. In fact, she was probably the most determined person her friends had ever met. "If you are constantly dwelling on something that happened in the past or feeling anxious about the future, you are missing out on YOUR LIFE," she wrote in her journal. "Do what makes you happy in the moment, and your life will be full."

Being part of the crew made Costello happiest. Cal head coach Dave O'Neill told her he would save her spot on the team. He didn't expect that she'd have the mental or physical strength to return, though. Yet by the following March, there she was at practice. She watched her teammates set out on a run. About a mile into it, they all took off their sweatshirts. Underneath, they wore yellow T-shirts that read CAL CREW CANCER KILLERS.

Costello continued to train with the team. It wasn't easy. She was always tired and in pain from her cancer treatments. But she pushed on. By May, the crew was getting ready for its conference championship. And Costello was in the running to serve as coxswain for the team's varsity boat. She had never done that before. O'Neill asked the eight varsity rowers to vote for their coxswain. They chose Costello. "Are you up for it?" he asked her. She smiled. "Yup."

LEAVING A LEGACY

Two weeks after the conference championship, Jill Costello led Cal's varsity eight-woman crew at the 2010 NCAA nationals. The team placed second. A month later, Costello died. But first she graduated, earning straight A's in her final semester. She also won an award as the most inspirational student-athlete at Cal. Her memory lived on when the Cal crew renamed one of its boats the *Jill Costello*. They wrote "Beat Lung Cancer!" on its side. Costello didn't win her battle with cancer in the end. But before she died, she organized a charity run called Jog for Jill. It eventually raised hundreds of thousands of dollars for cancer research. So her legacy may help defeat the disease after all.

When race day arrived, Cal's biggest rival was Stanford University. With only about 100 meters to go in the 2,000-meter race, Cal had a slight lead. But then a couple of rowers got out of synch. The boat rocked. Despite having a sudden bloody nose—not to mention a swollen belly and painfully puffy feet—Costello grabbed a rope and yanked hard. She put the boat back on course. Then she shouted two words that would echo in the ears of the Cal rowers. They went on to win the championship by the slimmest of margins. All the while, they marveled at their teammate's determination to fight until the end. All Costello said was, "Finish strong."

COURAGEOUS STAND

OCTOBER 16, 1968 • MEXICO CITY, MEXICO

For athletes, there may be no moment more glorious than winning an Olympic medal. After long, diffi cult years of training and competition, it's a dream come true. But it can be even more than that. In 1968, two men were brave enough to use their moment of glory to send a message. They stood up for what they believed while they stood on the medal podium.

That year was filled with conflict and tragedy. Civil rights leader Martin Luther King Jr. was assassinated. So was presidential candidate Robert F. Kennedy. Tens of thousands of people, including thousands of U.S. soldiers, were being killed and injured in the Vietnam War. Riots erupted in some American cities. Violent conflict between police and protesters had also recently taken place in Mexico City. That was where the Summer Olympics were taking place. So maybe it wasn't surprising that a protest became a lasting symbol of those Games.

On October 16, Tommie Smith won the 200-meter dash. He also set a world record time of 19.8 seconds. His American teammate, John Carlos, finished third. Gold and bronze medals were draped around their necks. Then they decided to turn their moment of celebration into a statement.

The two runners were both members of the Olympic Project for Human Rights. This group spoke out against the poor treatment of African Americans. A college professor named Harry Edwards had encouraged all African-American athletes to stay home from the Olympics. In the end, however, the group decided that each athlete would protest in his or her own way. Carlos said, "I had a moral obligation to step up."

Smith and Carlos knew what they wanted to do. When "The Star-Spangled Banner" began to play, each man bowed his head and raised a black-gloved fist in the air. This gesture symbolized the strength and unity of black Americans. Smith wore a scarf around his neck that represented black pride. The two athletes also wore black socks and no shoes to remind people that millions of African Americans lived in poverty. This symbol of resistance and defiance was called a "Black Power" salute. However, Smith didn't completely agree. He said it was really a "human rights salute."

The crowd booed as the athletes left the podium. The next day, the gesture was front-page news. Although some people supported Smith and Carlos, many others criticized them for making a political statement at the Olympics. (However, many countries have made statements over the years by refusing to take part in some Olympic Games.) The International Olympic Committee was especially upset. Its members

SILENT SUPPORT

A third athlete took part in that 1968 Olympic medal ceremony. It was the silver medalist, Peter Norman. He was a white Australian. After the race, Tommie Smith and John Carlos told Norman what they planned to do. He told them he supported their protest. And on the podium, he wore a badge in support of the Olympic Project for Human Rights. As a result, the Australian Olympic Committee punished him. Norman wasn't invited to be part of the 1972 Summer Games. Yet when he died in 2006, Smith and Carlos flew all the way from the United States to Australia. They helped carry his casket at the funeral.

suspended Smith and Carlos from the American team and sent them home. Back in the United States, Smith and Carlos faced racist comments and other abuse. Their families received death threats.

Smith went on to become a physical education professor and a public speaker. Carlos became a high school guidance counselor. Yet as the decades passed, Smith and Carlos earned respect for standing up for their beliefs in a nonviolent way. Years later, the college they both attended—San Jose State University in California—honored them with a 22-foot-high statue. Forty years after their protest, Smith and Carlos received the Arthur Ashe Courage Award. Their salute had become a symbol of the civil rights movement. And they were praised as two athletes who placed their principles above personal glory. Carlos looked back on that moment with pride and also surprise. He said, "I had no idea the moment on the medal stand would be frozen for all time."

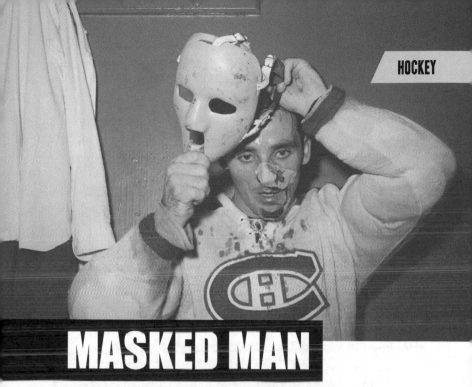

MASKED MAN

NOVEMBER 1, 1959 • NEW YORK CITY, NEW YORK, UNITED STATES

Many people would say being a goaltender in the
National Hockey League is courageous enough. Former
NHL goalie Brian Hayward once described his job: "It's
all about doing whatever you can to stop the puck.
You try to make yourself as big as you can and hope
that it hits you somehow." Hayward played for the
Anaheim Ducks. That team name describes how many
of us might react to a hard slab of rubber speeding
toward us. *Duck!*

But believe it or not, goalies didn't wear protective masks for many years. That didn't change until a man named Jacques Plante dared to try something different.

Plante was one of the top goaltenders in NHL history. He holds the record for winning the Vezina Trophy seven times. During his career, it was awarded to goalkeepers of the team allowing the fewest goals during a season. He recorded 82 shutouts in his long career, which lasted from 1952 to 1975. In 1978, he entered the Hockey Hall of Fame.

Over the years, Plante had worn a mask in practice once in a while. But he'd never worn it during a game. Hockey players are famous for being tough guys. Wearing a mask? In those days, people thought that was wimpy. It would take the league's most respected goaltender to change that thinking.

On November 1, 1959, Plante's Montreal Canadiens were playing the New York Rangers at Madison Square Garden. A Rangers player made a shot that hit Plante just below his left eye. He needed seven stitches to close the gash. That was a turning point. Between periods, Plante talked to his coach, Toe Blake. Plante told Blake he wouldn't play anymore unless he could wear a mask.

Plante's teammate, Hall of Famer Maurice "Rocket" Richard, remembered the moment. "Blake didn't like the idea of goalies wearing masks. It just wasn't done in those days. But there was nothing Blake could do," Richard said. "He let Jacques finish the game with that big thing over his face."

That "big thing" was a cream-colored plastic mask. It became a permanent part of Plante's equipment. Before that, many goalies had resisted wearing masks. For one thing, they were embarrassed to try it. But they were also afraid of hurting their game. They figured masks would make it hard to see the ice as clearly. But Plante was just as successful with the mask as without it. In fact, other goalies started to see that wearing a mask made it easier to tend the goal. In hockey, split second timing can make all the difference. With his mask, a goalie could watch the puck longer. He could stay on his feet more often. He could even use his face to stop a shot.

Today, all hockey players wear some sort of head and face

protection. Goalies wear up to 40 pounds of equipment. They even decorate their masks with wild designs meant to strike fear into opponents. But one player's courage to shrug off a fear of ridicule transformed the game forever. Jacques Plante changed the face of hockey.

GLOVE STORY

Long before Jacques Plante wore hockey's first goalie mask, Doug Allison took a similar step in baseball. Allison was a catcher on the first pro baseball team in the United States, the Cincinnati Red Stockings. He was also the first known player to wear a baseball glove. In baseball's early days, players fielded without gloves. But during a game in 1869, Allison hurt his hand. To protect it, he decided to wear a plain leather glove with the fingers cut off. It had far less padding than the catcher's mitts used today. But it was far more than anyone used back then. Baseball would never be the same.

REVEALING HER VOICE

SEPTEMBER 2011 • DUNSANY, IRELAND

Swedish golfer Sophie Gustafson has won more than two dozen professional tournaments. She has achieved great success. But she has done so very quietly. That's because she has a severe stutter. A stutter breaks up the flow of speech in various ways, making it difficult to finish words and sentences. Experts estimate that more than 70 million people around the world have stutters.

"For most people who stutter, the more comfortable they are, the better they speak," she said. "If you put us up in front of people, I guarantee that we will all struggle." For that reason, in 13 years as a pro, she had never done a television interview. Not one. But during a golf match in Ireland in September 2011, Gustafson made a courageous decision. She came up with a plan to speak for herself. The Golf Channel set her up in a room with a camera. There was no audience. Gustafson had a list of written questions. All she had to do was read them and answer them. Simple, right?

She began, "I wanted to go a little out of my comfort zone this year and just see if I was able to do it. So if you'll bear with me, you'll find out a little bit more about me." It took her several minutes to say those two sentences. In all, it took Gustafson about 70 minutes to answer a handful of questions. It took a Golf Channel editor more than two hours to create a

smooth three-minute interview. But the response was
overwhelming. Gustafson
heard from people all over
the world who were inspired
by her bravery. Some of
these people had stutters
themselves. Others didn't.
Afterward Gustafson said, "I
had no idea that this interview would stir up so many
emotions in people."

WISE WORDS

"To watch people push
themselves further than
they think they can, it's
a beautiful thing. It's
really human."
—Abby Wambach, soccer
player, coach, and two-time
Olympic gold medalist

Emotions were even stronger about seven months
later. That's when Gustafson won the Ben Hogan
Award. Each year, it's given to a person who stayed
"active in golf despite a physical handicap or serious
illness." Gustafson rose to accept the award. And a
room full of 350 people wondered what would happen next. They watched, many of them teary-eyed, as
Gustafson stood near a video screen. She'd recorded
her speech ahead of time. "I hope we can all agree that
this is the best way of doing this if you want to get out
of this room before the first tee time tomorrow morning," she said in her speech. Gustafson's talk showed
her typical sense of humor. But it was also serious.
"I've always stuttered," she said. "It's part of who I am.

Sometimes the words flow better, and sometimes they don't flow at all."

The speech lasted 6 minutes and 35 seconds. It took Gustafson *eight hours* to record it. She explained why she worked so hard at the task. "If I can help get the word out there about stuttering, then that's what I should strive to do," she said. "If I can use golf as a platform to raise awareness about stuttering and even help one kid feel better about themselves, then it has all been worth it."

Gustafson's wish came true very soon. She got a letter from the mother of a 12-year-old boy named Dillon. Dillon had a severe stutter. He was often ignored or bullied. He was very depressed. "Growing up I was lucky never to be teased," Gustafson said while receiving the Ben Hogan Award. "But I know a lot of kids with speech impediments get teased every day." There was a bright spot for Dillon, though. His school provided an iPad to help him communicate better. He worked hard and made the honor roll. He wanted to raise money to buy one for another classmate who stuttered. Gustafson asked her many blog and Twitter followers to donate to the cause. Within just 48 hours, they had raised enough money. Gustafson once said, "Maybe I can have an impact on people." She has.

FIRST AND FEARLESS

AUGUST 8, 1992 • BARCELONA, SPAIN

Hassiba Boulmerka was almost there. She had less than
a lap to go. She was racing in the 1,500-meter finals at
the 1992 Summer Olympics in Barcelona, Spain. And
she had just one runner to pass. The 24-year-old knew
that a gold medal was within her reach. It would be
the first ever earned by an athlete from her country.

Compared to all the obstacles she had overcome just to compete, this almost seemed easy.

Boulmerka was from Algeria. In this North African nation, Islam is the main religion. Many Algerian Muslims have strong beliefs about women and their clothing. They believe that when women are in public, they should be covered from head to toe. Boulmerka was a Muslim herself. She viewed Islam as a religion of peace and tolerance. But as a top athlete, she also needed to be competitive. Covering her arms and legs would slow her down.

Some strict Muslims thought women shouldn't be athletes at all. Only a few years earlier, a group of Algerians had tried to ban women from playing any sports. The ban didn't happen. But female athletes still faced big challenges.

Eventually, training in Algeria became dangerous for Boulmerka. As she jogged down roads, men would spit or throw stones at her. She ignored them and kept moving. But it was impossible to ignore *her*. In 1991, she became the first woman from an African or Arabic country to win a world track championship.

Many people hailed Boulmerka as a national hero for Algeria. They saw her as an inspiring symbol for women everywhere who hoped for more freedom. Yet some Muslims continued to speak out against Boulmerka. They criticized her because she "ran with naked legs in front of thousands of men."

When Boulmerka started to get death threats, she moved to Europe to keep training. When she arrived in Barcelona for the 1,500-meter finals, armed guards walked her to the stadium to protect her. But by the time she crossed the finish line, she was all alone. With 200 meters to go, she passed a Russian runner and glided to the gold medal.

When the race was over, Boulmerka raised a fist in the air. "It was a symbol of victory, of defiance," she later said. "It was to say: 'I did it! I won! And now, if you kill me, it'll be too late. I've made history!'" Still, she was proud of doing it for her country. She pointed to the colors of her nation's flag on her uniform and cheered, "Algeria!"

Boulmerka went on to compete in the 1996 Summer Olympics. After that, she retired from racing.

However, she kept working for the rights of female athletes. "There are women everywhere who would like to run but are afraid," she said.

Boulmerka received a high honor by being elected to the Athletes' Commission of the International Olympic Committee. She used her position to pressure governments that she believed discriminated against female athletes. Her work and her courage as a pioneer are paying off. In 2012, for the first time, *every* team that competed in the Olympic Games included at least one female athlete.

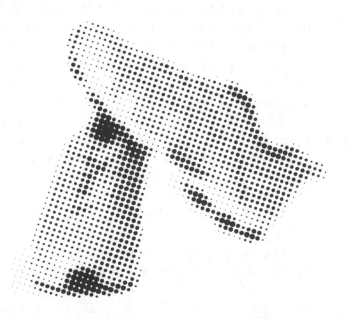

DRESSED FOR SUCCESS

Like Boulmerka, Bilqis Abdul-Qaadir was a female Muslim athlete. And like Boulmerka, she was taunted for how she dressed. Abdul-Qaadir was on her high school basketball team in Springfield, Massachusetts. When she played, she covered her arms and legs completely. She also wore a headscarf called a hijab. Some fans of opposing teams shouted at her. They called her names like "terrorist."

Other people simply asked Abdul-Qaadir honest questions about her religion. She was happy to answer. But perhaps her best answer was on the court. She became the first high school player in the state to score at least 3,000 career points. She earned a scholarship to the University of Memphis. She also received an invitation to dine at the White House. "Bilqis is an inspiration not simply to Muslim girls," said President Barack Obama. "She's an inspiration to all of us."

HURRICANE

1995 • NEW YORK CITY, NEW YORK, UNITED STATES

Some athletes show courage by overcoming injury and achieving excellence. Some are brave pioneers who break sports barriers. Others are heroic away from the athletic fields, helping people through hard times. Orlando Antigua was a bit of all three.

Antigua was born in the Dominican Republic. His father was Dominican, and his mother was Puerto Rican. He grew up in the Bronx section of New York City. On Halloween night in 1988, Antigua was the victim of a drive-by shooting. The person who shot Antigua thought he was someone else. A bullet went into Antigua's head, near his left eye.

Remarkably, Antigua recovered from the shooting. In fact, he was back playing basketball—his favorite sport—only two weeks later. Even more amazing? The bullet was still in his skull. Doctors didn't think it was safe to remove it until several years later.

Meanwhile, Antigua shone on the basketball court. He earned All-America honors as a senior. He was also student council president. On top of all that, he worked to be strong for his two younger brothers. Antigua helped keep his family together during a time when they were homeless.

Where did Antigua's courage come from? Some may have come from the shooting itself. Antigua always said that the experience changed his view of life. "You have the option of looking at it two ways," he explained. "You can say, 'woe is me' and not gain anything from it. Or you can be appreciative of the fact that you do have a second chance and try to do something with the second chance you've been given."

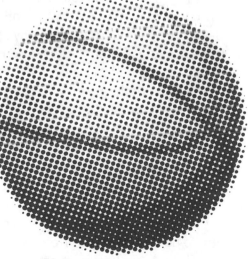

One big chance Antigua got was a college education. He earned a scholarship to the University of

Pittsburgh. The 6-foot-7 forward was the basketball team's captain for two years. He ranked among the school's all-time leaders in three-point field goals and blocked shots. He also spent summers playing in both his parents' homelands. He even played for the Dominican national team. In 1994, the United States Basketball Writers Association honored Antigua with its Most Courageous Athlete award. And all the while, he still had that bullet in his head.

After graduation, Antigua considered several offers. A few NBA teams invited him to attend tryout camps. Some European scouts told him he might have a future playing basketball overseas. Instead, in 1995, he took a chance and did something nobody expected. He accepted an invitation to play for the world's best-loved basketball team—the Harlem Globetrotters. The team is based in New York City and dates back to 1927. The Globetrotters nicknamed Antigua "Hurricane" for his quick feet and dazzling moves.

Antigua made history by joining the Globetrotters. He was the first Latino player ever to suit up for the team. He was also the first non-black Globetrotter in more than 50 years. "The Globetrotters were a great experience," he said. "I got to travel the world and entertain people. Not many people get that opportunity to be an ambassador of goodwill."

Antigua spent seven years with the team. He visited 49 countries. In his travels, he met many inspiring people, including South African President Nelson Mandela and boxing legend Muhammad Ali. Then he traded his red, white, and blue uniform for a suit and tie. Antigua became an assistant coach at several schools, including Pittsburgh. He also coached at the University of Kentucky, where he was one of the nation's top basketball recruiters. "I like to treat people well and do good work," he said, "and take advantage of whatever opportunities come my way."

WISE WORDS

"If you're willing to put yourself and your dreams on the line, at the very least you'll discover an inner strength you may not have known existed."

—Kurt Warner, former NFL quarterback and Super Bowl XXXIV MVP

THE PROTECTOR

JUNE 26, 2005 • BERKELEY, CALIFORNIA, UNITED STATES

It was after midnight on June 26, 2005. Mike Tepper was enjoying the summer after his freshman year at the University of California, Berkeley. That night, Tepper was walking home with a female neighbor. A carload of men cruised slowly alongside the pair. The men started to harass Tepper's friend. Some even tried to pull her into the car. Tepper, who stood 6-foot-6 and weighed more than 300 pounds, immediately tried to protect her. As an offensive lineman on a very good football team, protection was his responsibility on the field. Off the field, it was his instinct.

As Tepper and his friend walked behind the car, the driver slammed the car into reverse. Tepper lunged to avoid the car. At the same time, he swung his right arm to push his friend out of the way. She escaped with only a few cuts and bruises. Tepper wasn't so lucky. The car knocked him down. It rolled over his right leg, near the ankle. As Tepper lay on the ground, he saw an awful sight. The driver changed direction and started forward, right toward him. Once again, Tepper felt the car thump over his leg. He dug his fingers into a sewer grate to avoid being dragged down the street.

People often say that in moments like that, their lives flash before their eyes. That's exactly what happened to Tepper. He thought of his parents and his longtime girlfriend. He was glad to be alive. But when he looked at his leg, he wasn't sure how *long* he could live. His injury was gruesome. His lower leg was broken in four places. The bone was sticking through the skin. And he was losing a lot of blood.

Luckily, an off-duty police officer was only a block away. She called for help. Tepper survived, and doctors saved his leg. But they told him if he walked again, that would be something special. If he could run again, that would be amazing. Playing football again? That was unlikely.

Tepper's dreams of the NFL were crushed. He grew very depressed. He dropped out of school for a semester. People kept telling him he was a hero, but he didn't *feel* heroic. "I didn't know what to do. I was so confused," he said. "I was lost, completely not myself."

That's when he did another courageous thing: He got counseling. It can be difficult to ask for help. But

Tepper knew he needed to talk to someone. And it *did* help. "There are some things you can't handle on your own," he said. With time, Tepper's emotional injuries healed. So did his physical ones. Within four months, he was out of a wheelchair. He even did some jogging. And in 2007, he went back to school and played in 13 football games. Tepper missed the 2008 season with a different injury, but came back again the following

UNDAUNTED UMPIRE

For 14 years, Steve Palermo was an umpire in the American League. He was ranked first in overall performance. Everything changed in July 1991. Palermo was at a restaurant in Dallas, Texas. He suddenly realized that two waitresses were being mugged outside. When he ran out to help, he was shot. The bullet entered his spinal cord. He was instantly paralyzed from the waist down.

Doctors told Palermo he would probably never walk again. But after rehabilitation, he was able to walk using a leg brace and a cane. And at Game 1 of the 1991 World Series, Palermo threw out the ceremonial first pitch. He went on to be a supervisor of umpires for Major League Baseball. And in 1994, Palermo won the Arthur Ashe Courage Award.

year. He played so well that he was selected to the all-conference team. He would later live his NFL dreams after all, playing six games with the Indianapolis Colts.

After his final season at Berkeley, Tepper was named the team's Most Courageous Player on Offense. That night in the street, he had played defense. The courage part just came naturally.

LOST NO MORE

AUGUST 2008 • BEIJING, CHINA

In 1985, a baby boy was born in the tiny village of Kimotong, Sudan. The baby's parents named him *Lopepe*. They never could have known that they chose the perfect name. In the family's language, it means "fast."

The boy came to be known as Lopez Lomong. He lived in a mud hut with no electricity or running water. His village didn't have a school. And by the age of six, Lomong no longer even had his family. A group of soldiers stormed the village church one day and kidnapped dozens of children. The men threw Lomong into the back of a truck, which sped away from his helpless parents. The soldiers were in the People's Liberation Army (PLA). This group was fighting in Sudan's civil war. The PLA kidnapped children and trained them as soldiers. These children came to be known as the Lost Boys of Sudan.

The future looked dark for Lomong. But one day, he followed three older boys. They escaped the PLA camp by crawling through a hole in a fence. "We ran for our lives," Lomong said.

For three days and nights, the boys moved as fast as their bare feet could take them across the African plains. Finally they reached the border of Kenya. People there took the boys to a refugee camp called Kakuma. It would be Lomong's home for the next decade. "Life was hard," said Lomong. He slept in a hut with 10 other boys. He did his schoolwork by writing in the dust with his fingertips. But he also found a way to cope with his situation. "My only escape from everything that was going on around me was getting a chance to run," said Lomong. He often ran—in bare feet—18 miles around the edge of the camp. "When I ran," he said, "I was in control of my life."

One day, Lomong discovered the Olympic Games. He had never seen a television, and he'd never heard of the Olympics before. But that day, he and some friends walked five miles to watch the 2000 Summer Games. They viewed the Games on a black-and-white TV powered by a car battery. Lomong saw American sprinter Michael Johnson earn a gold medal.

As Lomong walked back to camp, he kept thinking about Johnson. He said to himself, *I want to run with those same three letters across my chest: USA.*

It seemed like an almost impossible dream. But the next year, Lomong got a chance at a new life. He was one of 3,500 Lost Boys who were brought to the United States. Lomong went to live with Barbara and Robert Rogers in Tully, New York. And he soon became a track star. He led his high school to a state title. Next he earned a scholarship to Northern Arizona University. In 2007, Lomong became an NCAA champion. That year he also became something far more important to him: a U.S. citizen.

In 2008, Lomong achieved his dream. He earned a spot on the U.S. Olympic team. He would eventually reach the semifinals of the 1,500-meter run in Beijing, China. But his finest moment came a few days before he competed. The members of the U.S. team voted on who would carry the American flag during the Opening Ceremony. They chose a former Lost Boy who had found a brighter future.

BRINGING HOPE HOME

Lopez Lomong became a U.S. Olympian again in 2012. This time he competed in the 5,000-meter run in London, England. He finished in 10th place. Before he made the trip to London, however, he returned to his native village of Kimotong. There he was finally reunited with his parents.

A lot had changed since the day the PLA had taken Lomong. After the civil war, Sudan split into two countries. Lomong's family now lived in South Sudan. The poverty Lomong saw in his homeland troubled him. He vowed to improve living conditions there. He started an organization called 4 South Sudan. This group focuses on helping the country in four areas—education, nutrition, health care, and access to clean water. Lomong's mission is to bring his native country the kind of hope and opportunity he found in the United States.

A FIRST BASEMAN'S FAREWELL

JULY 4, 1939 • NEW YORK CITY, NEW YORK, UNITED STATES

The story goes that Wally Pipp had a headache. So on July 1, 1925, the New York Yankees' starting first baseman was taken out of the lineup. He would never start another game for New York. Why? Because his replacement was a fellow named Lou Gehrig.

WISE WORDS

"To uncover your true potential you must first find your own limits and then you have to have the courage to blow past them."

—Picabo Street, Olympic-gold-medal-winning skier

Gehrig went on to play in 2,130 straight games. It was a record that stood until Baltimore Orioles shortstop Cal Ripken Jr. broke it nearly 60 years later. Gehrig smashed 493 home runs, had 1,995 runs batted in, and retired with a .340 career batting average. He ranks among the best sluggers in baseball history.

But in 1938, when he was only 35 years old, Gehrig started to slow down. He had only four hits in the team's first eight games. He struggled to field ground balls. He was worried that he was hurting his team. So he decided to take himself out of the starting lineup. As the Yankees captain, he took the lineup card to the umpires at home plate before the game in Detroit on May 2. For the first time in 13 years, his name wasn't on the list. When the Detroit fans learned the news, they gave Gehrig a standing ovation.

Six weeks later, on Gehrig's 36th birthday, doctors told him what was wrong. They had learned why he couldn't work wonders on the baseball field anymore.

Gehrig had a disease called amyotrophic lateral sclerosis (ALS). It causes the body's muscles to get weaker and weaker. Lou Gehrig was slowly dying.

On July 4, Gehrig's team held Lou Gehrig Appreciation Day at Yankee Stadium. Everyone from New York City's mayor to team groundskeepers gave him presents and trophies. Gehrig immediately set these gifts on the ground. He was too weak to hold them. Yankees manager Joe McCarthy gave a speech. He called Gehrig "the finest example of a ballplayer, sportsman, and citizen that baseball has ever known."

Now, it was Gehrig's turn to step up to the microphone. At first, he was too tearful to speak. Finally, in front of the quietest 61,808 spectators ever to fill a baseball stadium, he began. "Fans, for the past two weeks you have been reading about the bad break I got. Yet today, I consider myself the luckiest man on the face of the earth."

These words are some of the most famous in all of sports history. They are also some of the bravest.

Gehrig went on to thank the fans for their support through the years. He also thanked the owners of the Yankees, his manager, and even opposing teams. Finally, he spoke about his family. "When you have a father and mother work all their lives so that you can have an education and build your body, it's a blessing," he said. "When you have a wife who has been a tower of strength and shown more courage than you dreamed existed, that's the finest I know." Gehrig concluded, "I might have been given a bad break, but I've got an awful lot to live for."

Gehrig died less than two years later, at the age of 37. It was 16 years to the day since he replaced Wally Pipp. Soon, he was elected to the National Baseball Hall of Fame. He was also the first baseball player to have his uniform number—number 4—retired. And today, ALS is better known by another name. In a tribute to one man's grace and courage, it's called Lou Gehrig's disease.

SELECTED BIBLIOGRAPHY

Arnold, Chloë. "Hassiba Boulmerka: Defying Death Threats to Win Gold." www.bbc.co.uk/news/magazine-16962799. February 11, 2012 (accessed May 21, 2014).

Ballard, Chris. "The Courage of Jill Costello." Sports Illustrated. September 29, 2010.

Crouse, Lindsay. "For Runner with M.S., No Pain While Racing, No Feeling at the Finish." The New York Times. March 3, 2014.

Ellis, Jessica. "Lopez Lomong: From War Child to U.S. Olympics Star." edition.cnn.com/2012/08/06/sport/lopez-lomong-lost-boy. August 9, 2012 (accessed May 21, 2014).

Fixler, Kevin. "Shooting for Perfection." www.sbnation.com/longform/2012/12/13/3758698/rick-barry-underhand-free-throw-nba. December 13, 2012 (accessed April 28, 2013).

Herzog, Brad. "A Home Run for the Ages." Sports Illustrated. April 1, 1996.

Keown, Tim. "Road Tested." ESPN The Magazine. November 6, 2006.

Paese, Gabrielle. "Antigua Breaks Ground for Latinos in NCAA Basketball." Puerto Rico Herald. July 25, 2003.

Settimi, Christina. "Before Title IX There Was Maria Pepe Waiting His Turn at Bat'." www.forbes.com/sites/christinasettimi/2012/06/24/before-title-ix-there-was-maria-pepe. June 24, 2012 (accessed May 21, 2014).

Smith, Gary. "Remember His Name." Sports Illustrated. September 11, 2006.

Villegas Gama, Karla. "Sophie Gustafson: The Golfer Who Overcame a Stutter." edition.cnn.com/2011/11/30/sport/golf/golf-gustafson-stutter-solheim/index.html. November 30, 2011 (accessed May 1, 2013).

Younge, Gary. "The Man Who Raised a Black Power Salute at the 1968 Olympic Games." www.theguardian.com/world/2012/mar/30/black-power-salute-1968-olympics. March 30, 2012 (accessed March 22, 2013).

INDEX

Interior photo credits: Dot pattern images created by Michelle Lee Lagerroos; page 4: © Bettmann/Corbis / AP Images; page 10: AP Photo/West Hawaii Today, Michael Darden; page 13: based on a photo by © Martinmark/Dreamstime. com; page 14: AP Photo/Susan Ragan; page 18: based on a photo by © Parker Knight; page 19: AP Photo/Jeff Chiu; page 21: based on a photo by © Betochagas13; page 23: based on a photo by © Janece Flippo; page 24: AP Photo/James Crisp, File; page 29: based on a photo by © Anke Van Wyk/Dreamstime.com; page 30: AP Photo/Chris O'Meara; page 32: based on a photo by © Alexander Pladdet/Dreamstime.com; page 35: based on photos by Dru Bloomfield and © Ariwasabi/Dreamstime.com; page 37: based on a photo by © Darren Brode/Dreamstime.com; page 38: AP Photo/Elaine Thompson; page 42: © Bettmann/Corbis / AP Images; page 45: based on a photo by Frédéric de Villamil; page 48: AP Photo; page 50: based on a photo by Ryan Fung; page 53: © Bettmann/Corbis / AP Images; page 59: based on a photo by © JET Photographic; page 62: AP Photo; page 67: © Bettmann/Corbis / AP Images; page 69: based on a photo by © Mikhail Grushin/Dreamstime.com; page71: Press Association via AP Images; page 72: based on a photo by © Bowie15/Dreamstime.com; page 75: AP Photo/John Giles; page 76: based on photos by Dru Bloomfield and © Ariwasabi/Dreamstime.com; page 78: based on a photo by © Oleksandr Kalyna/Dreamstime.com; page 81: based on a photo by © Alexander Pladdet/Dreamstime.com; page 84: AP Photo/John Sommers II; page 88: based on a photo by © Cherezoff/Dreamstime.com; page 89: AP Photo/Kevin Frayer; page 91: based on a photo by © Flashon Studio/Dreamstime.com; page 93: © Bettmann/Corbis / AP Images; page 95: based on a photo by © Stuart Monk/Dreamstime.com

Brad Herzog is the author of more than 30 books for children, including more than two dozen sports books. He has also published three travel memoirs in addition to a fourth book for adults, *The Sports 100*, which ranks and profiles the 100 most important people in U.S. sports history. For his freelance magazine writing (including *Sports Illustrated* and *Sports Illustrated Kids*), Brad has won three gold medals from the Council for Advancement and Support of Education. Brad travels all over the United States visiting schools as a guest author. His website, **bradherzog.com**, includes information about his other books and about his school visits and presentations. Brad lives on California's Monterey Peninsula with his wife and two sons.

Find great sports stories
in all the

COUNT ON ME
Sports books

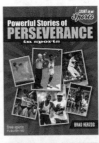
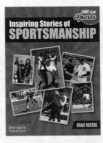

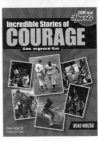

Download a **free leader's guide** at freespirit.com.

Encourage enthusiasm for reading and inspire positive character development with these powerful stories that highlight character building in sports. Each book features a wide variety of historical and contemporary stories of male and female athletes from around the world. The Count on Me: Sports series demonstrates the power and inspiration of true character. For ages 8–13.
Paperback; 104–112 pp.; 2-color; B&W photos; 5⅛" x 7"

Interested in purchasing multiple quantities and receiving volume discounts?
Contact edsales@freespirit.com or call 1.800.735.7323 and ask for Education Sales.

Many Free Spirit authors are available for speaking engagements, workshops, and keynotes. Contact speakers@freespirit.com or call 1.800.735.7323.

www.freespirit.com